HAL•LEONARD
INSTRUMENTAL
PLAY-ALONG

AUDIO
ACCESS
INCLUDED

PLAYBACK+
eed • Pitch • Balance • Loop

FLUTE

Disney

THE

LION KING

T0082041

Audio arrangements by Peter Deneff

To access audio visit:
www.halleonard.com/mylibrary

Enter Code
6523-7645-9717-6979

ISBN 978-1-5400-6562-9

HAL•LEONARD®

Visit Hal Leonard Online at
www.halleonard.com

Contact us:
Hal Leonard
7777 West Bluemound Road
Milwaukee, WI 53213
Email: info@halleonard.com

In Europe, contact:
Hal Leonard Europe Limited
42 Wigmore Street
Marylebone, London, W1U 2RN
Email: info@halleonardeurope.com

In Australia, contact:
Hal Leonard Australia Pty. Ltd.
4 Lentara Court
Cheltenham, Victoria, 3192 Australia
Email: info@halleonard.com.au

CONTENTS

CAN YOU FEEL THE LOVE TONIGHT

Flute

Music by ELTON JOHN
Lyrics by TIM RICE

CIRCLE OF LIFE

Flute

Music by ELTON JOHN
Lyrics by TIM RICE

HAKUNA MATATA

Flute

Music by ELTON JOHN
Lyrics by TIM RICE

I JUST CAN'T WAIT TO BE KING

Flute

Music by ELTON JOHN
Lyrics by TIM RICE

HE LIVES IN YOU

Flute

Music and Lyrics by MARK MANCINA,
JAY RIFKIN and LEBOHANG MORAKE

THE LION SLEEPS TONIGHT

Flute

New Lyrics and Revised Music by GEORGE DAVID WEISS,
HUGO PERETTI and LUIGI CREATORE

NEVER TOO LATE

Flute

Music by ELTON JOHN
Lyrics by TIM RICE

STAMPEDE

FLUTE

Composed by HANS ZIMMER

SPIRIT

Flute

Written by TIMOTHY McKENZIE,
ILYA SALMANZADEH and BEYONCÉ